YORK NOTES

William Wordsworth
Selected Poems

Note by Sarah Gillingham

York Press

ESSEX COUNTY LIBRARY

Sarah Gillingham is hereby identified as author of this work in accordance with Section 77 of the Copyright, Designs and Patents Act 1988

YORK PRESS
322 Old Brompton Road, London SW5 9JH

PEARSON EDUCATION LIMITED
Edinburgh Gate, Harlow,
Essex CM20 2JE, United Kingdom
Associated companies, branches and representatives throughout the world

First published 1999

ISBN 0-582-38198-3

Designed by Vicki Pacey
Phototypeset by Gem Graphics, Trenance, Mawgan Porth, Cornwall
Colour reproduction and film output by Spectrum Colour
Produced by Addison Wesley Longman China Limited, Hong Kong

ONTENTS

Preface   **5**

PART ONE

INTRODUCTION   How to Study a Poem   **7**
William Wordsworth's Background   **8**
Context & Setting   **11**

PART TWO

SUMMARIES   General Summary   **14**
Detailed Summaries, Comment,
Glossaries & Tests   **14**
SECTION I
Lines Written in Early Spring   **14**
Expostulation and Reply   **15**
The Tables Turned   **15**
Animal Tranquillity and Decay   **16**
The Reverie of Poor Susan   **17**
The Thorn   **17**
We Are Seven   **18**
Simon Lee   **19**
The Idiot Boy   **21**
Goody Blake and Harry Gill   **22**
Tintern Abbey   **23**
SECTION II   **27**
Lucy Poems   **27**
'Strange Fits of Passion have I Known   **27**
'I Travelled Among Unknown Men   **27**
'Three Years She Grew   **28**
'She Dwelt Among the Untrodden Ways   **28**
'A Slumber did my Spirit Seal   **29**
Lucy Gray, or Solitude   **30**
Nutting   **31**
'A whirl-blast from behind the hill'   **32**
Michael   **33**
Resolution and Independence   **35**
I Wandered Lonely as a Cloud ('Daffodils')   **37**
SECTION III   **40**
Composed upon Westminster Bridge   **40**

'It's is a Beauteous Evening'   **40**
The Solitary Reaper   **41**
She was a Phantom of Delight   **42**
Ode: Intimations of Immortality   **43**
SECTION IV: The Prelude   **46**
Book I   **47**
   'Fair seed-time had my soul'   **47**
Book II   **48**
Book III   **49**
Book IV   **49**
   Poetic Dedication   **49**
Book V   **50**
   'There was a Boy'   **50**
   The Nature of Poetry   **51**
   Visionary power   **51**
Book VI   **51**
   Crossing the Alps   **52**
Book VII   **52**
   London Images   **53**
Book VIII   **54**
Book IX   **55**
Book X   **56**
   The French Revolution   **57**
Book XI   **57**
Book XII   **58**
Book XIII   **59**

PART THREE

COMMENTARY   Themes   **61**
Form   **66**
Language & Style   **67**

PART FOUR

STUDY SKILLS   How to Use Quotations   **69**
Essay Writing   **70**
Sample Essay Plan & Questions   **73**

PART FIVE

CULTURAL CONNECTIONS
Broader Perspectives   **75**

Literary Terms   **77**
Test Answers   **79**

PREFACE

York Notes are designed to give you a broader perspective on works of literature studied at GCSE and equivalent levels. We have carried out extensive research into the needs of the modern literature student prior to publishing this new edition. Our research showed that no existing series fully met students' requirements. Rather than present a single authoritative approach, we have provided alternative viewpoints, empowering students to reach their own interpretations of the text. York Notes provide a close examination of the work and include biographical and historical background, summaries, glossaries, analyses of characters, themes, structure and language, cultural connections and literary terms.

If you look at the Contents page you will see the structure for the series. However, there's no need to read from the beginning to the end as you would with a novel, play, poem or short story. Use the Notes in the way that suits you. Our aim is to help you with your understanding of the work, not to dictate how you should learn.

York Notes are written by English teachers and examiners, with an expert knowledge of the subject. They show you how to succeed in coursework and examination assignments, guiding you through the text and offering practical advice. Questions and comments will extend, test and reinforce your knowledge. Attractive colour design and illustrations improve clarity and understanding, making these Notes easy to use and handy for quick reference.

York Notes are ideal for:
- Essay writing
- Exam preparation
- Class discussion

The author of this Note is Sarah Gillingham. Sarah studied English at St Hugh's College, Oxford University, and then worked for several charities. In 1988 she trained as a teacher, and since then has worked in FE colleges, most recently in Devon. She has taught English from basic skills to degree level, to all kinds of students. She is also an A level examiner.

The texts used in this Note are *Selected Poems of William Wordsworth*, edited by Roger Sharrock, Heinemann, 1958; *William Wordsworth, The Prelude or Growth of a Poet's Mind* (Text of 1805), edited by Ernest de Selincourt, corrected by Stephen Gill, Oxford University Press, 1970; *Lyrical Ballads* (Longman annotated texts), edited by Michael Mason, Longman, 1992 and *The Poetical Words of Wordsworth*, edited by Thomas Hutchinson, revised by Ernest de Selincourt, Oxford University Press, 1904.

> *Health Warning:* This study guide will enhance your understanding, but should not replace the reading of the original text and/or study in class.

EXPOSTULATION AND REPLY

THE THORN

PART ONE

INTRODUCTION

HOW TO STUDY A POEM

This book will help you to study the Selected Poems of William Wordsworth. These notes will supplement work you do in class.

- Reading poetry is quite different from reading a novel or a play. Except in a few cases, there is no plot to urge you to read on, to see what happens next.
- Instead of a cast of characters, there is just the poet and you, the reader. This is a one-to-one relationship in which you have to try to share the emotions that inspired the poem and that are expressed by the poet through words, but also indirectly through language and **rhythm** (see Literary Terms).
- The **form** (see Literary Terms) of a poem is important, as the poet chooses a particular form because it fits with the mood or message they want to create. It may seem like hard work at first, but as you become more skilled at reading you will enjoy the varied techniques poets use to suggest meaning.
- After your first reading of a poem, make a note of your impressions, together with where the poem can be found. Reread your notes later. Often you will find your views change as you get to know poems better. Always try to read a poem first yourself, before consulting these Notes. Test your ideas against those in the commentaries.
- Remember that poems can have more than one meaning! The most important thing is for you to start to develop your own views.
- With older poems such as these, it is quite important to consider the time they were written in. Reading the notes in Context and Setting will help you to do this

Wordsworth lived through exciting times for poetry and for life in general. He lived through revolutions in France and America, and through great political change in Britain.

Early childhood

One of the facts that is very well known about Wordsworth is that he comes from the Lake District. He was born on 7 April 1770, in the Cumbrian town of Cockermouth, the second child in a family of four boys and one girl. His father, John Wordsworth, worked as an attorney for the local landowner the Earl of Lowther, but the family suffered some financial hardships because John Wordsworth was owed money by the Earl. When William's mother died in 1778, he was sent to the grammar school in Hawkshead, in the centre of the Lake District. This was a time of exciting exploration for the young boy, when he first had the freedom to explore the countryside, and roam by himself. This is the basis for the inspiration for much of his poetry, notably 'Nutting' and *The Prelude* Books I and II.

Cambridge

In 1783 Wordsworth's father died, and he was left in the care of his uncle. He was sent to Cambridge in 1787, in the hope that he would enter the Church. Academic study did not suit him, though. He felt 'I was not for that hour, / Nor for that place' (*The Prelude*, Book III, lines 80–1) and he spent most of his time starting to write poetry, and also reading for pleasure. He seems to have been trying to combine the knowledge of books with the emotions and sensitivity to Nature of his earlier life.

France

In 1790, Wordsworth first visited France. Travelling in those pre-Shuttle days was adventurous and not as easy as it is for us today, and Wordsworth was deeply impressed by his first sight of the Alps (see **sublime** in Literary Terms) He was also aware of the astounding political events of the revolution, and the euphoria of the population was contagious. He joined in celebrations to mark the anniversary of the fall of the Bastille. In 1791, Wordsworth returned to France, and became even more firmly committed to the cause of the revolution, which he discusses in *The Prelude* Book VI. At the same time, he met Annette Vallon, and entered into a passionate, but secret, relationship with her. In 1792, she gave birth to their daughter, Caroline.

Wordsworth left France later that year, apparently intending to return and marry Annette, and there is much speculation about why he did not. It may have been to do with the differences between them (Annette's family were royalists, while Wordsworth was a revolutionary) but in fact, political events overtook his personal life, and within months England and France were at war.

Wordsworth had divided loyalties – to the revolution, and also to England, and to the causes of social justice, and his loyalty to France faded as the revolution abandoned justice and fairness. He writes of his disillusion in *The Prelude* Book X.

Wordsworth and Coleridge

Much of Wordsworth's life so far had been a struggle financially, but in 1795 he had a stroke of luck when a friend left him some money. He moved to Dorset, and his sister Dorothy, of whom he was very fond, came to live with him. Dorothy had a passionate interest in Nature and the countryside, and her notebooks, and her enthusiasm, seems to have helped William recover from his disillusion. As well as Dorothy, William had other friends in the literary world who encouraged him to start writing again. The most famous is Samuel Taylor Coleridge, whom he first met in 1795.

In 1797, the Wordsworths moved to Alfoxden in Somerset to be nearer to Coleridge, in Nether Stowey. This was an intense and exciting time for the two poets, and in collaboration they began to work on the *Lyrical Ballads*.

Germany   The following year, the three of them travelled to Germany, Coleridge going to Gottingen, and the Wordsworths going to the small town of Goslar, where despite a bitter winter, William worked on many poems, including the first two books of *The Prelude*, and most of the 'Lucy Poems'. It is possible that the isolation, cold and loneliness that William and Dorothy felt during this winter, helped William to look again at his childhood and the fond memories of his Lake District past. Later he wrote:

> I travelled among unknown men,
> In lands beyond the sea;
> Nor, England! did I know till then
> What love I bore to thee. (Lucy Poems, '*I Travelled among Unknown Men*', lines 1–4)

This was a period of intense creative activity for both Wordsworth and Coleridge resulting, in 1798, in the publication of the radical volume *Lyrical Ballads*. This was a collection they had worked on together, initially wanting to compose the poems together (starting with the idea for 'The Ancient Mariner'), but eventually concentrating on their own separate strengths. The publication of this – by two practically unknown poets – turned out to be one of the most significant events of English poetry, challenging previous views of what was acceptable in poetry, and indicating what was to come.

Return to the   In 1799, the Wordsworths moved to Dove Cottage in
Lakes   Grasmere. William was seeking security and a more settled life after his earlier travels. He married Mary Hutchinson – an old school friend – in 1802. He worked on some of his most famous poems at this time, including 'I wandered lonely as a cloud', 'Michael', the first version of *The Prelude*, and the 'Immortality Ode'.

Over the next few years, Wordsworth's relationship with Coleridge deteriorated, as Coleridge's health and opium addiction affected him more and more. Wordsworth was also aware of his own ageing, and the loss of the intensity he felt when young. He started to feel he could only achieve happiness through controlling the emotions, and coming to terms patiently with life's troubles – the very opposite of what he and other **Romantic** (see Literary Terms) poets had felt earlier! He also started to become more conservative politically, and this was condemned by other poets, memorably Shelley, who said 'What a beastly and pitiful wretch that Wordsworth! That such a man should be such a poet!' At the same time, it is clear to us, as readers, that Wordsworth had lost the really great poetic ability that had sprung from those intense recollections of childhood and emotion.

CONTEXT & SETTING

Revolution-aries

Today we live in a time of dramatic change; new technology, new methods of communicating, the opportunity to travel relatively easily to new and exciting places. In many ways, the world Wordsworth lived in had many similarities.

Across Europe and North America, countries were starting to break old bonds and become independent nations and democracies, freed from the excessive power of monarchs. The American War of Independence had ended in 1783, and the French Revolution was in 1789. The same desire for freedom could be found in writing, too. Tom Paine's book *The Rights of Man* had been a bestseller in 1792, closely followed by Mary Woolstonecraft's *Vindication of the Rights of Woman* later the same year. Poets too were involved in these political revolutions. Wordsworth and

Coleridge were both strong supporters of the French Revolution, at least initially, while Shelley and Byron (later Romantics) were both supporters of revolutionary causes; Byron died in 1824, leading the 'Byron Brigade' in the Greek struggle to free themselves from Turkish rule.

Wordsworth's most explicit discussions on political revolution are in *The Prelude*, but it is central to our understanding of his work to know that, especially in the early years, he was part of a poetic revolution, which has continued to have an effect to this day.

Romantics

Put the idea of Barbara Cartland and love stories out of your head when you hear the word 'Romantic' from now on. The **Romantic** (see Literary Terms) movement was not about love, but it was about feeling and emotion in a way that felt very new at the time.

Earlier in the eighteenth century, poets had looked for beauty in order and control. You only have to look at some of Capability Brown's well-manicured gardens, or read Alexander Pope's controlled poems, to see that control of Nature, and sophisticated manipulation of complex language were the dominant ideas at the time. Partly as a result of boredom with these ideas, partly through excitement at the political revolutions occurring, things began to change.

A new language

Poets like Wordsworth, Coleridge, Blake and Burns rejected the overblown language of their predecessors, and looked for a language that ordinary people would enjoy. They listened to popular songs, **ballads** (see Literary Terms) and stories, and tried to introduce a feeling like this into their work. The 'Lucy' poems and many of Wordsworth's *Lyrical Ballads* are good examples of this. Wordsworth and the other Romantics wanted poetry to be accessible to ordinary people.

Intense
emotion

At the same time, ideas about intense emotions and feelings were also important, and the language had to reflect this. Much of the controversy about Wordsworth's writing stems from this. He wanted to express extreme emotion – like Johnny's natural joy in 'The Idiot Boy', the distress of the betrayed woman in 'The Thorn' – but was also struggling to write in the voices of people who had been excluded from poetry before.

Imagination

We take it for granted now that imagination, creativity and originality are good things. You might be surprised to hear that this was not really true before the Romantics. Some people are shocked when they find out that Shakespeare, for example, did not invent the stories or most of the characters in his plays. His audiences at the time would not have been shocked. They expected writers to do this. It was a writer's job to collect material, and present it in an entertaining way. What was new about the Romantics was that they valued creativity and originality, just as we do today, so Wordsworth and the other Romantics laid the ground work for the way we think about poetry today.

PART TWO

SUMMARIES

GENERAL SUMMARY

Many anthologies of Wordsworth's poetry are available. I have chosen a selection of poems which seem to me to be central to Wordsworth's reputation. Most of these are from the earlier period of his writing. I have included summaries and some excerpts from *The Prelude*. The spellings and line numbers for the majority of the poems are taken from the Sharrock edition; those for '*I wandered lonely as a cloud*' from the Hutchinson/Selincourt edition; those for *The Prelude* are taken from the Selincourt/Gill edition and those from the *Lyrical Ballads* 'We are Seven', 'Simon Lee', 'The Idiot Boy' and 'Goody Blake and Harry Gill' from the Mason edition. For further details see Preface

SECTION I

LINES WRITTEN IN EARLY SPRING (1798)

The poem reflects on the harmony of Nature, but this brings about inevitable thoughts of sadness. The poet contrasts the easy enjoyment which Nature seems to feel with the way that humans cause distress and disharmony.

COMMENT

Do you think the very obvious rhyme scheme works?

On one level this is a poem about disharmony, about the way that mankind is the one element which doesn't fit in to Nature's order. At the same time, Wordsworth is careful to make the poem itself very ordered, in terms of its rhyme scheme, and the repeated and controlled **diction** (see Literary Terms). He sees his role as a poet to mediate between Nature and other people.

This poem also uses an idea very common in Wordsworth, that natural objects can feel human

emotions, as he senses that even the twigs on the trees
feel pleasure as the breeze touches them. He feels
humans have lost this ability.

GLOSSARY   **sate** sat. Wordsworth is deliberately using a rather archaic word
here
periwinkle an old-fashioned plant, with trailing stems and bright
blue flowers

EXPOSTULATION AND REPLY (1798)

Notice how the character of each speaker is reflected in their style of speech.

A character whom Wordsworth calls Matthew scolds
Wordsworth for idly sitting around doing nothing,
when he should be reading and learning. Wordsworth
replies that he is learning more deeply by just sitting
and experiencing the beauty of Nature. He says that
stillness and calm are better ways of letting the mind
work, rather than forcing it.

COMMENT
Why do you think the words 'wise' and 'passiveness' are put together?

This and the following poem ('The Tables Turned') are
important because they clearly show us Wordsworth's
view of Nature and of the human relationship with it.
He values the senses and what we can learn through
experience rather than through the intellect.

GLOSSARY   **that light bequeathed / To Beings else forlorn and blind** books are
the only key to knowledge

THE TABLES TURNED (1798)

There is a very jaunty effect in this poem.

This time, it is William who scolds his friend, telling
him to get up and leave his books of philosophy and go
out and experience Nature at first hand.

COMMENT

Notice the pun in 'barren leaves'.

On the surface both of these poems are anti-
intellectual, in that Wordsworth seems to be rejecting
books and reading. He says that real contact with
Nature is more worthwhile than any amount of contact
with philosophers (sages).

In a way, though, he is only attacking what we might call a reductive intellect, which is so intellectual it misses the real point of things. He talks of 'Our meddling intellect' which 'mis-shapes the beauteous shapes of things', so he is really suggesting a greater openness of mind.

GLOSSARY   a vernal wood a wood in springtime
            We murder to dissect in our desire to understand things
            scientifically, we may end up damaging what we seek to
            understand

ANIMAL TRANQUILLITY AND DECAY (1798)

This describes an old man whom the narrator sees walking in a country lane. He seems to be the ideal image of a person truly at one with Nature.

COMMENT   In some ways this is a rather unsuccessful poem.

Be aware of how   It is typical, in that it describes a human being at the
listing is used to very edge of experience – poverty stricken and old.
create an image of
persistence.   This figure is also seen as being completely at one with
            Nature – like Lucy. The poem in earlier editions had
            this rather strange ending, which feels very prosaic, but

Wordsworth later omitted this, ending the poem with 'what the old man hardly feels' which seems more successful.

THE REVERIE OF POOR SUSAN (1797, PUBLISHED IN 1800)

This is a poem of longing and homesickness. Susan lives in the city of London, but each day she passes a thrush, singing at the corner of the street. The song of the thrush fills her with a vision of the hills, trees and mountains where she grew up.

COMMENT   This poem may remind us of Wordsworth's own periods of travel in Germany and France, and the isolation he sometimes felt there.

The poem is striking in its **form**, using rhymed **couplets** (see Literary Terms) and a distinctive **rhythm**, similar to that used in street **ballads** (see Literary Terms) and songs of the time.

The vision of the rural home she has left may remind us of the setting for the 'Lucy' poems, but the power of Nature to restore and comfort even from a distance is common in several other poems of this period.

GLOSSARY   **Lothbury, Cheapside** poor areas of London

THE THORN (1798)

What features of the 'loquacious' narrator can you detect?

The poem is in the voice of what Wordsworth calls 'a loquacious [talkative] narrator'. The narrator describes an old thorn bush, which looks neglected and abandoned. Next to it is a small pool, and a tiny, mossy hill. He also describes a woman who sits beside the pond. He tells the woman's story, of how she fell in love with Stephen Hill, but was jilted by him on her wedding day. The woman was pregnant, and the combination of the jilting and the shame has driven her mad. The narrator is unsure about what happens when the baby is born. He speculates that it was still born, but suspects (though this is unspoken) that the woman murdered the child, and buried it by the pool, and this feeling is shared by some of the local villagers.

Comment   This is a good example of a longer narrative poem, and also of a poem which experiments by trying to find language which would be accessible to ordinary readers.

Some people have found the simplicity of the language almost comical.

What impression does the final stanza make on you?

In fact, there is some underlying symbolism which works through the poem; all the red colours (e.g. the vermilion of the flowers, the red of the cloak) seem to suggest an act of violence or tragedy.

Wordsworth is always very keen in comments to separate himself from the character of the narrator, and this reminds us that the narrator is not always the same as the author.

GLOSSARY   lichens small, grey, moss-like plants
cups flowers, blossoms
sober sad deeply serious, in contrast to her occasional madness
aver insist

We are seven (1798)

A narrator describes a meeting with a little village girl, who seems to him to embody childish charm and innocence. He asks how many brothers and sisters she has, and she replies that there are seven children in all, including two who have died and lay buried in the nearby churchyard. The narrator tries to explain that they are dead, and that there are only five children, and feels she is innocent or foolish in her disbelief.

COMMENT

Which is more convincing: the child's view, or the adult's?

Wordsworth is using two voices to great effect here. He uses the narrator to show the ignorance of one who cannot understand the child's organic relationship with Nature, and the child's clear voice and definite explanations show her view of the continuity of identity which lasts through death.

It is a touching image when the child describes how the dead are as real to her as the living, when she describes knitting and singing to her dead brothers and sisters. She is very matter of fact when she describes her sister Jane's death. She is unsentimental and clearly has no illusions about death, unlike the more squeamish-seeming narrator.

The simplicity of the language masks the more complex set of beliefs outlined in the poem. Wordsworth was warned before publication that people might be insulted by, or mocking of, this poem, but he insisted on its publication. There were similar doubts expressed about 'Simon Lee'.

GLOSSARY **porringer** a small plain bowl

SIMON LEE (1798)

How do we feel about Simon early on in the poem?

This tells the story of Simon Lee, who was once famed for his skill and strength as a huntsman. Now he is old and feeble, and has only a tiny plot of land to help support himself and his wife. He is so weak and close to death that his wife does most of the work on the land, of which he is ashamed. The narrator directly addresses the reader, accusing them of expecting some tale to be told. All that he tells is a single incident when the old man has long been trying to cut down an old tree, and the narrator helps him with a single blow, for which Simon is tearfully grateful.

COMMENT   In the Preface to the *Lyrical Ballads*, Wordsworth wrote
of his desire to show the concerns of 'low and rustic
life', and to make poetry (previously considered a highly
intellectual and primarily upper-class activity) more
accessible to ordinary people.

The strong rhyme pattern, simple structure and content
is striking in the poem, and a good example of
Wordsworth deliberately working with everyday,
accessible forms of the time. Many more intellectual
critics did not approve of these experiments, and
mocked Wordsworth for trying them.

Wordsworth shows he is aware of potential critics
waiting impatiently for him to say something profound,
when he directly addresses such readers in the eighth
stanza (see Literary Terms). He shows he is aware of
how impatiently these readers have waited for the real
point of the poem – and tells them they will be
disappointed.

Our response to the character of Simon Lee himself is
the key to the poem. At the beginning, with the
narrator, we seem to share a detached, unemotional
view of the character. We are aware of the change from
healthy strong young man to feeble old man, but
unmoved by this. We could argue that the trite and
simple language of much of the poem encourages us to
think like this.

Notice how your feelings change at this point. At the end of the poem, Simon's emotional response to
the simple act of help from the narrator transforms our
feelings. We are immediately sympathetic to the old
man, and now see him as an individual, suffering his
own personal tragedy.

Wider themes become apparent by the end of the
poem. The contrast (and gap) between youth and old
age is obvious, but we also see strong ideas about
harmony and gratitude.

Livery-coat uniform belonging to a particular aristocratic family
stone-blind so exhausted he can no longer see
stout strong
over-tasked have too much to do
thanks ... run so fast there is some irony in the suggestion that
Simon's thanks are now running as fast as he did in his
prime

THE IDIOT BOY (1798)

This is another narrative poem, again featuring characters from the margins of society. Betty Foy, a mother, has sent her son, Johnny, to fetch a doctor to help a neighbour, Susan. The narrative of the poem continually expresses doubt as to the wisdom of sending Johnny on such an errand, and it is made clear that Johnny is an 'idiot boy'. Johnny is excited by the idea of being on a pony, but does not seem to understand his mother's instructions, though she is proud and hopeful he will perform the errand. During a long night nursing Susan, Betty begins first to doubt, and then to worry

How do you think
Wordsworth
wants us to react
to Johnny?

about Johnny. Eventually she goes in search of him, asks the doctor where he is, but forgets to ask him to come to help Susan. As she is returning, fearing Johnny is lost or dead, she sees him, still on the pony, and she is delighted. As they return, she sees Susan, who has been so worried she forgot her previous illness. Johnny reveals his innocence and his lack of understanding of what has happened to him by his final comment.

COMMENT   Choosing a character like Johnny for a poem was a bold move on Wordsworth's part.

Yet again, he is choosing a character right from the margins of society, here, an 'idiot', whose mental capacities are not known.

Many people have seen this poem as an image of maternal love, observing the care and joy with which

The word 'idiot' has changed its meaning. Consider how.

Betty treats Johnny. At the same time, Johnny himself is important – the kind of intense joy he feels is an emotion which Wordsworth has in other poems identified as being precious, and also mainly associated with childhood.

Many **colloquial** (see Literary Terms) and regional phrases are used to give local colour to this poem – look at 'in this mighty fret', and 'fiddle-faddle' early on in the poem.

GLOSSARY   fret   fuss or panic

girt   girth

fiddle faddle   fuss

burr   a noise

hurly-burly   loud noise

merry tune   happy frame of mind

quandary   muddle, state of confusion

mischances   disasters, misfortunes

cattle   dialect word whose meaning included horses

hob nob   in cheerful company

fast she holds   to hold tightly

Goody blake and harry gill (1798)

This is a narrative poem, in a traditional style. We first meet the character of Harry Gill, who despite being young and strong is always cold. In contrast, Goody Blake is a frail old woman, who is so poor she never has enough wood to make a fire to keep warm in winter. We are then told the story of how she stole some old wood from Harry's hedge, and he caught her. When he confronted her, she prayed that he would never be warm again, and from the next day, her wish seems to be granted.

COMMENT   In many ways, this seems to be one of the most traditional poems in the *Lyrical Ballads*. It has a **form** which Wordsworth took directly from traditional ballads, using two identical quatrains (see Literary Terms). The colloquialisms (see Literary terms)which are introduced also give us a flavour of a rustic source.

In fact, Wordsworth's source for the story was Charles Darwin, who relates it in one of his books. It is unusual for Wordsworth to use an incident not witnessed by himself or a close friend.

Many people have commented on how frequently Wordsworth chooses to show a woman's point of view in his poems.

When Wordsworth and Coleridge began writing the *Lyrical Ballads*, one of the themes they wanted to address was the supernatural. In fact, although it might look as though the rather witch-like Goody has cast a spell on poor Harry, it is actually quite clear that Wordsworth's explanation is more psychological. He sees Harry's coldness as psychosomatic (created by his own imagination), and not a supernatural event at all.

Goody Blake is also one of the group of characters Wordsworth shows as suffering extreme deprivation – she is not only poor, she is much poorer than other poor people.

GLOSSARY   **Goody Blake** Goody is an abbreviation of 'goodwife', which was a term of address used for lower class housewives
lusty young and strong
drover Harry reared cattle and drove them to market
pottage a thin stew
canty cheerful

TINTERN ABBEY (1798)

How effective do you find the descriptions of Nature in the first section?

Wordsworth returns to the Wye valley, which he had visited five years previously. He looks out on the scene and is conscious of its wild beauty. Although he has been away, the memory of the scenery has stayed with him and sustained him in even the busiest of cities. He is, however, aware that his own response to Nature has changed over time, and feels a little sad and anxious that he has lost the youthful response, though he is also aware of the deeper pleasure his adult mind can gain out of community with Nature.

COMMENT

Look at the sets of adjectives in each section. Think about how they help you establish the tone of each part of the poem.

This is one of the most important of Wordsworth's poems to appear in *Lyrical Ballads*, but it presents an interesting contrast with other works there, because it does not shy away from using more complex language, and **diction** (see Literary Terms) which is self-consciously poetic. It was written a little later than most of the other poems in the edition.

Some of the syntax is far from the 'common language of man' advocated by Wordsworth in the Preface.

Look at, for instance:

> These beauteous forms
> Through a long absence, have not been to me
> As is a landscape to a blind man's eye

It is an explicitly **autobiographical** (see Literary Terms) poem – the first important one that Wordsworth wrote- and this shows Wordsworth's increasing interest in the inner life of the poet, which culminates in his writing of *The Prelude*.

Another central idea which increases in importance in this poem is the idea of memory, and the way that memory can be used as a force to transform the present. In some ways, Wordsworth seems to be arguing that events have a more powerful effect after having been filtered through memory.

In the poem, Wordsworth is accompanied, we learn at the end, by his sister. Dorothy, with her enthusiasm ('wild ecstacies'), seems to represent the younger William, before the moderating and deepening force of memory has had its effect.

What other poems contain this idea?

Tintern Abbey also shows Wordsworth beginning to contemplate his own death, as he asks Dorothy to be consoled by memories of him.

GLOSSARY

impress carries the meaning of impressing with their grandeur, but also literally pressing on – like pressing an image into wax

pastoral here means natural, uncultivated

evil tongues gossips

Identify 'who' or 'what' could be found at the following locations:

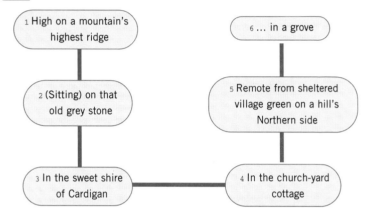

1 High on a mountain's highest ridge

6 ... in a grove

2 (Sitting) on that old grey stone

5 Remote from sheltered village green on a hill's Northern side

3 In the sweet shire of Cardigan

4 In the church-yard cottage

Check your answers on page 79.

Consider these issues.

a Why Wordsworth so often chooses rural working-class or poor people within these poems. Look for other later poems where he also does this.

b What you think it is possible to tell about Wordsworth's views on poetic **form** (see Literary Terms) and content from these poems?

c What reaction you think readers of Wordsworth's own time, used to high-flown poems about formal subjects, would have had to these poems.

d Choose a poem which seems to you to be most typical of Wordsworth's style at this time. Make a description of its characteristic features (look at the rhyme scheme and **versification**, the **rhythm**, the **diction**, the **tone**, the use of characters, the content and themes). Try to relate this poem to others he wrote at this time.

e Why some people have said that Wordsworth has a special sympathy with women. Choose two poems from this section and use them to consider this idea.

f Why poems like 'Simon Lee' and 'The Thorn' were felt to be over-simple by critics when they were first published. What do you think Wordsworth was trying to do when he wrote them?

Section II

Lucy poems (1798/9)

I. Strange fits of passion have I known

The narrator of this poem starts by celebrating his love for Lucy, waiting in her cottage for him. As he travels he watches the moon go down, he feels a sudden sense of anxiety (the 'Strange fits of passion' in line 1) and fears, for no logical reason, that she is dead.

COMMENT

Notice the connection between the rose, symbolising Lucy's beauty, and the moon, as it sinks in the sky.

The poem is written as a memory. Is Lucy alive or dead?

The 'Lucy Poems' are popular because of their apparent simplicity – the simple lyrical form (see Literary Terms), and also because of the strange and poignant feeling which lies behind them.

There is no explanation in the poem of why the Lover feels like this, and no sense of time to help us know what might happen in the future.

The poem ends in a melodramatic way. It is interesting to note that in an original draft version, there is another stanza (see Literary Terms), where it is made clear that Lucy has died. Wordsworth decided to leave the ending of the poem more open.

GLOSSARY   What once to me befell what once happened to me
lea meadow, field

II. I travelled among unknown men

This poem (written rather later than the others) reflects Wordsworth's increasing love for the English countryside, and his rejection of the restlessness which led him to travel.

The Lucy figure is part of an idealised landscape.

COMMENT   This poem is written two years after the others in the group, but we can still see the importance of the Lucy character as a symbol of beauty, Nature and harmony, associated specifically with the English countryside.

There is a typical Wordsworthian reference to childhood scenes implied in the second line of the last stanza.

GLOSSARY   **turned her wheel** the image is of Lucy spinning wool beside the fire – a comforting and domestic image

bowers the word suggests leafy green, sheltered areas

III. THREE YEARS SHE GREW

Consider why there are so many opposing pairs in the poem.

This poem is mainly spoken in the voice of Nature, who has chosen Lucy as a child of her own. We see the growth and progress of the young Lucy, under the guidance of Nature. At the end of the poem the time perspective changes again, and it is clear that Lucy is now dead.

COMMENT

Why do you think the idea of Lucy's death is so important in these poems?

This poem shows us the process of achieving harmony with Nature. Wordsworth imagines the growth of Lucy, helped by Nature. It is interesting that he draws attention to the fact that both sides of Nature, the beautiful (e.g. the fawn) and the dangerous (e.g. the motions of the storm) are used to shape Lucy's character. Many images are repeated within the Lucy group, including, here, the comparison with a flower.

GLOSSARY   **sportive** playful

IV. SHE DWELT AMONG THE UNTRODDEN WAYS

Are you shocked by the sudden reference to death in the final two lines?

This apparently simple little poem begins by describing the beauty of Lucy within her limited surroundings. Again she is compared to a flower. The final **stanza** (see Literary Terms) refers to her death.

COMMENT

The poem begins by emphasising Lucy's distance from other humans, and revealing her closeness with the natural world, again using simple **imagery** (see Literary

Terms) ('A violet by a mossy stone'). Some people have seen the image of the 'mossy stone' as suggesting Lucy's gravestone. Certainly the violet is a fragile flower. Again the images of the wider natural world – here of stars – are used.

The final stanza contains a change of mood. It begins by seeming flat and unemotional / down-to-earth in the first two lines, but introduces a very real sense of pain in the final line. Although we do not know very much detail about the character of the narrator (or of Lucy), the intensity of feeling is very convincing and personal.

The mention of 'Dove' at the beginning could refer to rivers in the Lake District, Yorkshire or Derbyshire. Perhaps Wordsworth was trying to make the meaning of the poem more general.

V.   A SLUMBER DID MY SPIRIT SEAL

The poem has the atmosphere of a dream, in which the narrator imagines Lucy, beyond death, and completely at one with Nature.

COMMENT

This is the shortest and most enigmatic of the 'Lucy Poems'.

What effect is achieved by the choice of the rather scientific word 'diurnal'?

It is far from simple, despite the excessive simplicity of the **form** (see Literary Terms). The fragile, flower-like Lucy of some of the other poems has become something with a quality beyond time, beyond the human. She is timeless and part of the whole scheme of Nature.

Interesting readings of the poem can show how looking at the two **stanzas** (see Literary Terms) separately can bring about different interpretations. The first stanza could be read as referring to Lucy before her death, the second after. Other readings look at both as a response to her death. The first would tend to make the poem feel depressing – the narrator was fooled into thinking Lucy was immortal and unchanging, but is shocked into the realisation that she is not by her death. In the second, there is a much more positive sense that death itself may be meaningful and a part of a real human relationship with Nature.

Wordsworth did feel this, but at the same time, his sensitivity to the pain death causes to the bereaved means that the meaning of the poem is probably open.

GLOSSARY   **A slumber did my spirit seal** describes a dream or trance-like
state, similar to the 'strange fits of passion'
diurnal daily

LUCY GRAY, OR SOLITUDE (1798/9)

Lucy is 'the solitary child'. Which other characters does she remind you of?

The character of Lucy Gray is introduced as another isolated, unworldly figure. Her father asks her to take a lantern out, to help light her mother home that evening. Lucy cheerfully does this, but that is the last her distraught parents see of her. They have just begun to accept that she must be dead, when they catch sight of her footprints, which they follow until they reach the middle of a bridge, when the footsteps stop suddenly.

COMMENT   This poem was based on a real event, in which the child's body was found. Wordsworth alters it so that there is a much more mysterious and less definite ending.

As with some other poems in this section, Lucy seems at one with Nature, and, in many ways her death is not regarded as a tragedy, except in the way that it affects her grieving family.

There is a somewhat ghostly sense here, of Lucy still
wandering the moor, emphasised by not finding her
body. This is unusual, in that, although Wordsworth
was passionately interested in the supernatural, and in
country ghost stories, he often shied away from using
them in his poetry.

It is worth noticing that the narrator catches sight of
Lucy 'at break of day', which is the same time as her
parents abandon hope of seeing her again.

NUTTING (1798/9)

This poem is in the form of a childhood memory. The
narrator recalls leaving the house when he was a boy, to
go and collect hazelnuts in the woods. Initially, he feels
intoxicated with the beauty of his surroundings, but his
mood changes, and for reasons he cannot explain, he
vandalises the trees. At the end, he seems to regret
what he has done.

COMMENT

*Many people have
noticed the sensual
or even sexual
quality of the
language here.*

This is one of Wordsworth's strangest and most
memorable poems. The early description is very typical
of other childhood memory poems, such as the early
books of *The Prelude*. The language is very sensuous,
concentrating on specific details of the landscape and
his response. It very vividly describes the young boy
setting out with energy and enthusiasm, and then
emphasises the sudden violence of his attack with heavy
rhythms and dull monosyllables (see Literary Terms)
('... earth ... branch ... bough').

The attack is explicitly described as a rape; the grove
was a 'virgin scene', his attack is a 'merciless ravage',
and afterwards the bower is described as 'sullied'
(dirtied) by his act.

There is a mystery (even to the narrator) about why he
commits this act of violence to the countryside he

seems to enjoy so much. We can understand this now
from the parallel experience of environmentalism – our
love for the beauty of the countryside may result in its
becoming spoilt and busy through overuse.

GLOSSARY   **sallying forth** going out (suggests hope and energy)
                nutting-crook a hooked stick to pull down the best branches
                cast-off weeds / Motley accoutrement old clothes

'A WHIRL-BLAST FROM BEHIND THE HILL' (1798, PUBLISHED IN 1800)

In the poem, a sudden rush of wind is described and
then a dramatic hailstorm. The poet is sheltered
amongst evergreen hollies and observes the way the
fallen holly leaves move and dance as a result of the
hailstorm.

COMMENT   The idea of natural objects being able to feel emotion,
                or at least have senses is very vivid here.

What effects are   Wordsworth uses **alliteration** and strong **rhythm** (see
achieved by using   Literary Terms) in the early part of the poem to
repetition in the   describe the 'whirl-blast'. The very strong rhyme
poem?   scheme in the poem also contributes to the sense of
                        rhythm.

There is a sense of the wonder of observation in the
voice of the narrator.

GLOSSARY   **Robin Good-fellow** originally the name of an evil demon. By
                Shakespeare's time this had come to mean a mischievous
                goblin or fairy. The character Puck in *A Midsummer Night's
                Dream* also refers to himself as Robin Goodfellow
                minstrelsy from the word minstrel, an old fashioned word
                meaning musician or singer, minstrelsy is used by Wordsworth
                to suggest the secret music to which the leaves are dancing

MICHAEL (1800)

The narrator introduces us to a wild and rugged landscape, and to a pile of stones he has seen there. He then tells us the story behind these stones. First he introduces the main character, Michael, an old shepherd, who is strong and healthy, despite his age (in his eighties). He has worked hard all his life to build up his farm, helped by his wife, Isabel, and, in later life, by their son Luke. The whole family are known for their industry. When Luke is 18 and Michael is looking forward to leaving the farm to him, they become responsible for the debt of another member of the family. Instead of losing the farm (and Luke's inheritance), the family decide that Luke should be sent away to work for a rich relative. As Michael says goodbye to Luke, he asks that Luke should lay the first stone in the new sheep pen he is building, which Michael will continue with, and which he hopes will be complete when Luke returns. Although things go well at first, Luke soon falls into bad company and eventually gets into so much trouble he has to leave the country. Michael and Isabel never see him again, and after their death, the farm is sold to a stranger.

COMMENT   Wordsworth described this as a 'pastoral poem'. The
           pastoral (see Literary Terms) was a style fashionable in
           classical and neo-classical (eighteenth century) times,
           where poets wrote about the countryside, often
           idealising it, and used ideas about the country to
           comment on the values of the city.

           Michael is not a traditional pastoral, therefore. The
           view of Michael, though admiring and respectful, is not
           idealised; he is a real countryman.

           Some critics suggest that Michael is based on Thomas
           Poole, a farmer who helped Wordsworth and Coleridge
           in their Somerset days.

           Michael is another Wordsworth character who is seen
           as being instinctively very close to Nature. His
           relationship is described as being 'a pleasurable feeling
           of blind love, / The pleasure which there is in life itself'
           (lines 76–7).

           The narrator is closer to Wordsworth's own character
           here than in some of the other narrative poems
           (compare this to 'The Thorn').

           There are several important symbols in the poem. For
           example, the lamp works as a symbol of the
           hardworking family (it is actually described as a 'public
           symbol' in the poem). The most important symbol,
           though is the sheepfold itself. Initially it is a 'covenant'
           between Michael and Luke, then as it remains
           unfinished, with Michael too old or too dispirited to
           complete it, it is a symbol of Luke's betrayal of the
           family trust.

Make a note of   The end of the poem is typically ambiguous. Although
any optimistic   there is a sense in which it is very bleak – the farm
elements in the   has been sold to strangers, and all Michael's and
poem.   Isabel's work was in vain – there is a hint of continuity,
                    not only in the unfinished sheepfold (which, you

will remember, inspired the memory of the narrator), but in the oak tree which still grows beside their door.

The poem is in the **form of blank verse** (see Literary Terms), such as that used throughout most of Shakespeare's plays. This forms a contrast with many of the more rhythmic and song-like poems which Wordsworth wrote at this time.

GLOSSARY   Greenhead Ghyll   a waterfall in the Lake District. Even though Michael may be based on a Somerset character, it is important for the drama and wildness of the setting that it be located in the Lakes

A story – unenriched with strange events   there was a fashion at the time for stories containing elements of the supernatural, as you can see if you read 'The Rime of the Ancient Mariner', Coleridge's poem in *Lyrical Ballads*. Wordsworth, however, felt uncomfortable with ideas about the supernatural, and therefore emphasises the reality of this story and writes in a naturalistic way

Resolution and independence (1802)

The speaker is travelling alone across the moors on the bright morning after a storm. Initially he feels uplifted by the vibrant weather, but suddenly he feels full of gloom and despair. He starts to remember the tragic lives of other poets, who died penniless. He meets an old man, whose poverty is obvious. He asks the man what he is doing, and the man replies that he is a leech-gatherer, although this work is now much more difficult than it was in the past, as leeches are more scarce. Wordsworth feels uplifted by his encounter.

COMMENT   This has many typical features of Wordsworth's poetry.

The old man is seen as elemental, especially on first meeting, when he could be mistaken for the rock on which he sits.

The poet is able to re-evaluate his own experience through his meeting with the leech-gatherer, impressed as he is by the man's ability to persist with his own life despite the difficulties.

This poem gives us a good chance to see how Wordsworth adapted material from his own life into poetry. The poem is based on an incident in his own life, but he made several changes. In the poem, he is alone, but in real life he was with Dorothy. He also changes the location. Instead of the reality where he met the old man on the road, in the poem he meets him in the middle of the moors. The most important change made, though, was that in reality the man had ceased to struggle with work as a leech-gatherer, and become a beggar. In the poem, Wordsworth emphasises the man's sense of pride and persistence.

The poem was written in 1802, though it was not published until five years later. In it we can see evidence of Wordsworth's growing doubts and anxieties about his own creative abilities, and about his ability to support his family through poetry. In fact, for many people this was the time that Wordsworth's creative talents did begin to decline, and the great creative period of his earlier life was, with a few exceptions, over.

GLOSSARY

Chatterton a boy poet (1752–70) who became famous for publishing supposed medieval poems, but which turned out to be his own work. He committed suicide in poverty in 1770, but became a hero of the **Romantic** (see Literary Terms) movement, for both his life and work

I WANDERED LONELY AS A CLOUD (COMMONLY KNOWN AS 'DAFFODILS') (1804)

The narrator speaks in the first person, describing first his (aimless) walking, then the sudden sense of surprise as he catches a glimpse of the daffodils. He compares their movement to the movement of water. He stares at the flowers in enjoyment. Afterwards, he realises that the memory of the flowers will stay with him forever.

COMMENT   This is probably Wordsworth's most famous poem. It is popular because it seems to sum up how we think poets ought to behave – they should wander round, their heads in the clouds, and should enjoy looking at flowers!

On a more serious note the poem returns, in a simpler way, to the idea in 'Tintern Abbey', that the power of a natural experience may not be obvious at first, but will powerfully remain with you, to be sought out by the 'inward eye' in future times.

The structure of the poem, though apparently simple, helps to reinforce the message. The echoes and repetitions or similar words (synonyms) in the language 'a crowd … a host', 'beside the lake … beneath the trees', 'fluttering and dancing' help to suggest the idea of an image returning later to us, perhaps not quite in the same form in which we experienced it originally. It certainly reminds us of Wordsworth's definition of poetry as 'emotion recollected in tranquillity'.

Consider other poems in which characters are closely linked with Nature.

Wordsworth very consciously links himself to the daffodils, counting himself as in their company.

The **couplets** at the end of each **stanza** (see Literary Terms) are very striking, and draw attention to the final two lines.

Stylistically, there are some interesting contrasts in the
diction (see Literary Terms) at the end, specifically the
movement from the poet on the 'couch ... vacant ...
pensive' to the sudden 'flash', and the apparent (but not
necessary) juxtaposition of 'bliss' and 'solitude'.

GLOSSARY   Milky Way a constellation of stars. It looks rather like spilt milk
             in the sky
             inward eye a famous phrase of Wordsworth's. It seems to be a
             combination of memory and imagination

A ... *Identify the person these phrases describe.*

1 ... she I cherished turned her wheel / Beside an English fire

2 – The sweetest thing that ever grew / Beside a human door!

3 ... a Figure quaint / Tricked out in proud disguise of cast-off weeds

4 An old man, stout of heart and strong of limb

5 His body was bent double, feet and head / Coming together in life's pilgrimage

6 He in the dissolute city gave himself / To evil courses

Check your answers on page 79.

B ... *Consider these issues.*

a The features the 'Lucy Poems' have in common with each other. Make a list of these features and consider whether they have features in common with other poems.

b Why 'Daffodils' is such a well-known poem.

c What connections can be made between the leech-gatherer in 'Resolution and Independence' and other characters in other poems.

d The attitude to childhood shown in several of Wordsworth's poems and compare them (include 'Nutting').

e How much sympathy we have with characters in Wordsworth poems. List what the poet does to help us sympathise and what he does to hold back our sympathies.

Section III

Composed upon Westminster Bridge (September 3, 1802)

This **sonnet** (see Literary Terms) describes a beautiful view of the city of London, seen early in the morning. The description concentrates on the fact that the normally busy city is calm and sleeping.

COMMENT
This is an unusual poem; it is one of Wordsworth's rare poems on a city, rather than on the rural landscape.

Here, the sonnet **form** lends itself perfectly to the meaning, with the **octet** (see Literary Terms) consisting of a description of the city, and its beauty. The **sestet** (see Literary Terms) moves the idea on, to show how a city, as well as the country, can be peaceful. The final three lines sum up the key images of the poem, with the river seeming like the guiding spirit of the city, and with the whole place being symbolised as a beating, sleeping heart.

'It is a Beauteous Evening' (1802)

Another sonnet, this time set in the evening. The sun is going down and there is a real sense of an eternal presence. The poet is walking with a young girl, and observes the inner divinity that is within her.

COMMENT
This poem is interesting primarily because the little girl is Caroline, Wordsworth's illegitimate daughter. He had gone to see Caroline and her mother, Annette Vallon, in France in 1802, just before his marriage to Mary Hutchinson.

The poem reminds us in some ways of the 'Lucy Poems', with the 'eternal motion' of God, and also the way that the innocent child can somehow be closer to God and Nature than adults.

THE SOLITARY REAPER (1805)

The poem observes a woman working alone in the fields. As she works she sings in Highland Gaelic. The writer wonders what she is singing about, and finds the sound of the song very haunting and moving, even though he cannot understand what it means. The song stays with him even after he can no longer hear it.

COMMENT   In 1803, Wordsworth had travelled with Dorothy to Scotland, and this was one of a number of poems inspired by this visit, though he had also read a travel book, 'Tour in Scotland', by Thomas Wilkinson, which may have given him the idea.

Wordsworth uses old-fashioned language to suggest the rural setting and the sense of time past.

A typical Wordsworthian idea is shown here; the idea of things lingering on after they have gone. This is a familiar theme – consider the 'Lucy Poems' and 'Tintern Abbey'. The fact that the song is in Gaelic (which Wordsworth does not understand) is also interesting, as it reminds us that we may feel emotions even though we might not understand why.

The figure of the solitary reaper herself is one of many solitary figures in Wordsworth's poems.

The strong **rhythm** and obvious rhyme scheme in the poem are used to suggest the idea of sound; the rhymes of the two last **couplets** in each **stanza** (see Literary Terms) perhaps suggesting the echo of her song around the valley.

GLOSSARY   numbers the verses of her song
                  lay a traditional song
                  sickle a tool used when reaping

SHE WAS A PHANTOM OF DELIGHT (1804)

This is a poem about the poet's wife, Mary.

It starts by describing how she first appeared to him, and uses images of brightness and stars to show her appearance to him. He calls her both a perfect woman, and a perfect spirit, combining the human with the spiritual.

COMMENT   The use of **imagery** (see Literary Terms) is much more notable here than in many of Wordsworth's early poems. Mary is compared to stars and other natural features as a way of showing her beauty, but also her quality of something beyond the human.

At the same time, Wordsworth sees her as very human; she is 'A creature not too bright or good / For human nature's daily food'. We might see a contrast with the earlier and highly idealised figure of Lucy.

The use of the word 'machine' is an eighteenth-century usage. It means organism or whole, rather than the modern, technical meaning.

Identify the lists The poem lacks some of the earlier intensity of the
which Wordsworth Nature poems, and this is reflected in the rather list-
uses in the poem. like style of parts of the description.

ODE: ON INTIMATIONS OF IMMORTALITY FROM RECOLLECTIONS OF EARLY CHILDHOOD (1802-4)

Consider the function of the three-line stanza at the beginning.

Notice the symbols from the natural world which Wordsworth uses.

Look at how rhythm might be used to suggest meaning in these stanzas.

This Ode sums up the emotions of doubt and unhappiness Wordsworth is feeling, but it also examines the sources of inspiration.

In the first and second stanzas (see Literary Terms), Wordsworth admits that his ability to perceive has changed, as time has passed, and that, despite the beauty of the natural world, 'the things which I have seen I now can see no more'. He regrets the loss of artistic vision.

In stanza III, he feels he is excluded from the unity of Nature, though in the next stanza he claims to still feel included.

In stanzas V, VI and VII, he tries to explain the process by which this loss of intensity occurs.

In the eighth stanza the poet directly addresses a child, and asks them not to be in a hurry to put childishness behind them.

By the ninth stanza, Wordsworth is attempting to work out what is left for the adult mind in terms of consolation. Although intuitive unity with Nature may not be possible, it is possible for the adult to understand intellectually, and to remember, and this more mature, if less intense, reflection must be the consolation of the adult.

COMMENT

This Ode is the key poem of Wordsworth's later period, though, in fact it was begun as early as 1802. It explains in poetic terms what he feels is happening, but it also has a quality of controlled emotion, which was to be what Wordsworth sought to communicate in his later work, and which is, perhaps, the reason why the later work, with its tone of resignation, is less popular, and less successful, than the earlier.

This must be one of the most painful poems for a writer ever to have written. The poem is heavy with the sense that the pure inspiration, the clear vision of the child has gone forever.

According to Dorothy, the first four stanzas were written in 1802. The struggle with changing emotions is already obvious. The poem places vivid experiences in the past ('There *was* a time', 'It is not now as it hath been of yore' – emphasis added). Notice how Wordsworth deliberately uses the archaic word 'yore' to suggest past time, even though this was a word he would normally rarely use. This combines effectively with use of the past tense.

Early on in the poem, it seems as though Wordsworth is trying to persuade himself that he still be a part of the unity of Nature: 'The fulness of your bliss, I feel – I feel it all', but it is difficult not to notice the hesitation and doubt in that repetition.

The **imagery** (see Literary Terms) of the poem also strongly supports the meaning. The strong cosmic and natural images at the beginning, the joyful **pastoral** (see Literary Terms) references in stanzas III and IV, and perhaps most poignantly, the image of 'embers' in IX, which is all he has left of the vivid fires of inspiration.

Even by Wordsworth's time, the Ode was an old-fashioned **form** (see Literary Terms), rarely used. He chose to employ it here because it gave him some flexibility in manipulation of the form and length of the stanzas. Notice, for instance, the first fairly short, elegant stanza, which sums up the whole meaning of the poem in its long last line.

A

Identify the person 'to whom' these comments refer.

> 1 A Spirit, yet a Woman, too!

> 2 ... Single in the field

> 3 Dear child! dear girl!

> 4 A six years' Darling of a pigmy size

Check your answers on page 79.

B *Consider these issues.*

a What points Wordsworth is making about poetry and emotion in the 'Intimations' Ode.

b In the light of your answer to **a**, make a visual plan which shows the progression of thought in the Ode.

c Whether you think there is any progression between the earlier poems and these later works. Consider:
– themes and concerns
– form
– language and style
– imagery and symbolism
– attitude to Nature and to people.

d How effective you find the imagery and symbolism in this group of later poems, for example the embers in the Ode, the star and light imagery in 'She was a Phantom of Delight'.

e Whether you find any interesting similarities or differences between 'She was a Phantom' and the 'Lucy Poems'.

Section iv: the prelude

The Prelude (1799–1805 though Wordsworth continued to make revisions to it all his life)

Introduction

Obviously *The Prelude* is much too long a poem to deal with in depth in a study guide of this length. I will summarise the key points of each Book, and also take a look at one or two of the better known sections in detail.

How does Wordsworth's use of time compare with any other autobiographies you have read?

The books are roughly chronological, in that they describe Wordsworth's life and poetic development in an approximately logical way. Typically of Wordsworth, though, they all contain elements of memory, so even in the later books you will find him referring back to important childhood experiences which have remained with him. This is central to his idea that the roots of his poetic abilities are based on these childhood experiences.

The poem is addressed to Coleridge (it was mainly written before their terminal argument), and Wordsworth sometimes contrasts his experience with that of the other poet.

The subtitle of the poem, 'The Growth of a Poet's mind' was extremely original in its time. There was no history of poets looking closely at their own experience, with a view to explaining their work. This was pre psychoanalysis!

Do you think it helps you to understand poetry if you know more about the poet's ideas?

Wordsworth (in the preface to a later poem, 'The Recluse'), described how he wanted to 'take a review of his own mind, and examine how far Nature and Education had qualified him for such an employment [as a poet]'. He saw the poem as only an introduction(!) to the planned work, 'The Recluse', though in fact he never completed this last work. He says *The Prelude* 'conducts the history of the Author's mind' up to the point where he felt he could enter 'upon the arduous labour which he had proposed to himself'.

Book i: introduction - childhood and school-time

What techniques does Wordsworth use to evolve the idea of childhood?

This tells the history of Wordsworth's early childhood, and contains some key episodes, and some of the best-known parts of the poem. It would have been a very unexpected read at the time – this concentration on the key points of your own poetic development back into childhood was unusual. You can see this concentration on his own development very clearly in this section.

'Fair seed-time had my soul' (lines 305–489)

In this section, Wordsworth sees early childhood as a preparation for becoming a poet. He describes his childhood with great affection, and with a fondness for the freedom he had then. He tells of the freedom to roam, day and night, in the countryside. He parallels the emotions of beauty (which he sees in the countryside), and fear (of discovery if he poaches from someone else's trap). There is a sense of himself as a child interacting with Nature, as he watches the clouds in line 350. He reflects on the way the human mind has an inner harmony, like music, which he can now detect, in adult life.

The most famous section begins 'One evening' (line 372), and tells the strange story of a time when the young poet steals a boat to row out on the lake of Patterdale. (The modern equivalent might be joy-riding!) He describes the guilt he feels, but also the pleasure. As he rows the boat out on to the lake he suddenly becomes afraid – part of the cliff beside the lake seems to come to life and rear up and threaten him, as though it is alive. Terrified, he returns the boat to its place, but he is haunted afterwards by the memory of it.

The mood here is of fear, and of a sense of the terrifying power of Nature.

Another well-known section begins at line 452, when, even though it is cold and after dark, he has such pleasure in skating on the lake. He vividly describes the scraping, tinkling sound of the skates on the ice.

Book II: School-time (continued)

You will notice that most of the memories connected with school are not of the academic life. Instead, Wordsworth remembers going riding, being outside, walking. He does revel in the actual experiences of these brushes with Nature, but he also says 'I still retained / My first creative sensibility ... My soul was unsubdued. A plastic power abode with me; a forming hand' (lines 378–82). He already had a strong sense of his own creative potential.

Look at the section lines 292–307 to see a discussion of Wordsworth's relationship with Nature.

He thanks Nature in the poem for providing him with the potential for inspiration, and for providing him with a kind of central security 'in thee, / ... I find a never-failing principle of joy / And purest passion' (lines 463–6).

He refers directly to the contrasting experience Coleridge must have had, brought up in the city (London), but states that they have both come to share their appreciation of Nature.

GLOSSARY   plastic flexible and creative. Wordsworth intended to give the sense of a potential for creativity

Book iii: residence at cambridge

Early in this section, lines 97–120, Wordsworth describes how his mind ran more on to higher things.

Wordsworth looks back on his first term at Cambridge with mixed feelings. He feels some pleasure, notably at the discovery of the pleasures of human company – he had previously been a very solitary individual, and is pleased to discover some sociability (lines 216–36). He feels uncomfortable about his studies, and spends his time reading Chaucer, Spenser and Milton instead (lines 276–293).

He did not enjoy his studies in general, and worries that he was not really suited to Cambridge: 'A feeling that I was not for that hour / Nor for that place' – he also says in lines 506–7 that he did not love 'the guise Of our scholastic studies'.

Book iv: summer vacation

Wordsworth returns from his first year at Cambridge and describes with pleasure his first view of his beloved Lakeland. His time away has somewhat altered him, and he is able to look anew at characters who were formerly familiar to him, particularly the old dame with whom he lodged at school. He describes how he sees these characters 'with another eye' (line 205). He still feels that the attractions of sociability are distractions, but feels he has overcome this, when, after an all-night party, he returns home through the dawn, and feels a promise has been made, committing him to a life dedicated as a poet. In the final part of the Book, he meets a veteran soldier, destitute, and assists him.

Poetic dedication (lines 316–45)

Notice the key passage where Wordsworth describes a solitary night.

The earlier lines here remind us of Wordsworth's discovery of the delights of a social life which he described in Book III. There is often an ambiguity in his pleasure. In some ways, his enjoyment of the party seems to enhance his appreciation of Nature, and it is at this point that he formally dedicates himself to Nature and to poetry.

His dedication is made and acknowledged to Coleridge in line 340.

BOOK V: BOOKS

This section begins with Wordsworth's concern about how the relics of the human race, particularly works of artistic creation, will last through time. He recounts a mysterious dream, of the figure of an Arab man on a camel, inspired by having read Don Quixote. The figure seems to represent a kind of leader whom Wordsworth can follow.

Look back to the Lucy Poems for more ideas about Nature and Childhood.

The poet also expresses his opposition to ideas about education which involve cramming the young mind with theories (lines 295–349), and abandoning the wonders of Nature. This section includes a very famous part of the poem, 'There was a boy', and this links to his dramatic memory of having once seen a dead body dragged from the lake. He also links this incident to his creative debt to the stories and tales of imagination which are often despised by 'intellectuals'.

'THERE WAS A BOY' (LINES 389–413)

This section describes how the 'boy' who has a close relationship to the young Wordsworth, goes out into the country and mimics the noise of owls hooting. This sets up an echo.

This section shows once again Wordsworth's sense of how close the young can get to a real relationship with Nature. As the boy imitates the owl, he himself becomes a part of the whole of Nature. He is described as an 'instrument' for a voice more powerful than his own. The owls themselves answer, responding to his call, and this communication echoes around the whole valley. Much of the language seems to include ideas of response and answering. Even when he gets no reply from the owls, the very being of Nature seems to enter into his spirit. This shows a good example of Wordsworth exploring the idea of human unity with Nature.

THE NATURE OF POETRY (LINES 516–57)

Wordsworth here explores the idea of poetic inspiration, particularly through the value of the simpler sorts of literature – popular folk tales and fiction, for which he says we still have an appetite.

VISIONARY POWER (LINES 608–29)

What other Wordsworth poems refer to this idea of 'visionary power'.

Wordsworth here makes a link between Nature and the finest poetry. He writes of 'the great Nature that exists in works/Of mighty Poets' (lines 618–19), and says that there is some similarity between the forces of Nature and the forces of creativity.

BOOK VI: CAMBRIDGE AND THE ALPS

The 'Fellow Student' (line 339) is Wordsworth's long-standing friend, Robert Jones.

This section outlines two important and contrasting sections of Wordsworth's youth. First, his continuing studies as Cambridge, including the pleasure he gains from Mathematics, but also the way he is aware of the growth of his own 'poet's mind' during this time. This was the beginning of the period of Wordsworth's European travels, and he also makes a dedication to Coleridge at this point, comparing Coleridge's experience of growing up in the city with Wordsworth's own childhood, and also acknowledging their similar poetic destiny.

Wordsworth describes how moved he is by the beautiful scenery of the Alps, and describes how this scenery stimulates and lifts up his imagination.

CROSSING THE ALPS (LINES 525–72)

Wordsworth crossed the Alps on foot in 1790 during a walking tour. In the past, he had written more soberly about the experience, but now he seems to be transfixed by the intensity of his experience. He seems to feel his reactions are so intense that they bring him into contact with feelings which are beyond the natural – almost divine.

BOOK VII: RESIDENCE IN LONDON

Notice the use of sound in much of this section, e.g. lines 184–204.

The first part of this book is spent reintroducing the idea of inspiration through Nature, represented here by the song of the robin.

The most important part of this book, though, is written about Wordsworth's time in London. Wordsworth was poor at this time, so he spent hours wandering the streets, just looking at people. He paints a rich picture of the variety of life in London – as in so many of his poems, he is interested in those on the margins – the poor, the abused, the lonely or the strange. He describes many of these people, including especially the Maid of Buttermere, a Lake District woman who was deceived by a man, and who bore him an illegitimate child. This had been made into a stage musical at the time, but Wordsworth still manages to suggest compassion and sorrow for the real woman herself. Other characters he notices with sympathy include beggars, prostitutes, street sellers and entertainers. He vividly describes the exotic wonders of the Bartholomew Fair. The only characters he shows no sympathy for are the lawyers and politicians.

Towards the end of this section, Wordsworth considers the relationship between the country and the city. This has often been a theme in poetry, but Wordsworth changes the focus by concentrating on the nature of inspiration in both places, and he says that he believes that the same force of Nature which inspires him in the country, also reaches him in the city. He writes of the 'Spirit of Nature' and 'The Soul of Beauty and enduring life'.

LONDON IMAGES (LINES 595–741)

This is the section where the poet describes himself going through the streets, and then experiencing the Bartholomew Fair, and finally where he reflects on the continued power of Nature to affect him even when in the city.

The overall impression given by this section really sums up the busy and vibrant streets of London as they would have been at this time. Much of the writing is rather list-like, helping to give the impression of the many and varied sights the poet is experiencing for the first time.

Wordsworth tries to refer to all the senses in his description.

Although the subject matter – life in the city- is unfamiliar, we can still see many features of Wordsworth's writing which are typical of his more usual style and concerns. The most obvious idea here is his interest in the people on the margins of society, for example in line 612, where he observes the 'blind Beggar'.

There are differences however. Wordsworth in London is acutely aware of life as a pageant, or stage show, passing before his eyes. This image is made more strong by many references to the stage and acting. He explores this idea in lines 618 onwards, where he suggests that people in extreme circumstances can help us to see the deep reality of human nature and meaning.

The most important section in terms of the themes of *The Prelude* as a whole is the final ten lines, where he once again returns to the idea of Nature as a unifying force, visible in even the most unlikely environments.

Wordsworth lived in London relatively early in his career, and it is almost as though he is consciously using the experience of living in a large, unfamiliar city to test out his ideas about poetic inspiration, to see whether they still work in an atmosphere so very different from his beloved and familiar Westmorland hills.

BOOK VIII: RETROSPECT

Look at
Wordsworth's
comparison of
town and country
in lines 62–6.

This book illustrates the complex way in which Wordsworth deals with time in *The Prelude*, and shows that the organisation is not in a clear chronological timeline from childhood to the experience of the adult poet. Instead the poem moves through time, referring backwards to memory, and forwards to future experience. Book VIII is an excellent example of this, (Retrospect means a look backwards) as here Wordsworth goes right back to look through his life so far, in order to tell where his poetic inspiration, and his love of Nature and humanity has come from.

*Wordsworth
creates a sense of
the real Lake
District landscape
in lines 222–45.*

At first, he is very conscious that his first love was for Nature. As he grows older, he recounts stories that show his gradual realisation of his equal love for humanity. One important story here is that of the Straggler of the Flock, which helps him to see human love. Many of his early stories are of shepherds, and he contrasts these real, down-to-earth workmen with the idealised and unrealistic shepherds of literature, such as those in Shakespeare's *As You Like It*. At the end of the section, he has looked back over his whole life up to the point of his time in London, and he has gradually realised that his pure love for Nature has not been replaced by love for humanity, but that the two are now equal in his mind.

Book IX: RESIDENCE IN FRANCE

At the start of this section, Wordsworth re-establishes the time scheme, by stating that, at the end of a year in London, he decided to move to France, mainly to improve his French.

*Notice how
Wordsworth uses
the image of a
flowing river to
describe the rather
random progress of
the poem.*

He describes Paris, and shows awareness of revolutionary events, but does not really take them seriously at this stage, enjoying viewing paintings more. He moved to Orleans, and later to Blois, though there is no distinction made between the two in *The Prelude*.

He describes how republicanism comes naturally to him, born as he was in a simple down-to-earth area, and how Cambridge taught him to respect people for their abilities and achievements, not their titles. His awareness of the revolutionary cause develops slowly, but accelerates as his friendship with Beaupuy, a soldier loyal to the revolution, develops. He describes how influential this friendship was for him. The rest of the Book is taken up with the story of Vaudracour and

Julia, which he says Beaupuy told him. It is a tragic tale where two lovers, of slightly different class, are forbidden marriage by the parents. The woman bears a child, and is sent to a convent never to see her lover or her child again. The man determines to look after the child himself, and, although he has a nurse to help him, kills the child 'by some mistake or indiscretion'. He lives a life of tragic isolation for the rest of his days.

In many ways this tragic love story is the only hint Wordsworth gives of his own passionate love for Annette Vallon. Critics sometimes say that the excitement of the early courtship of the two lovers in the poem is symbolic of William and Annette's relationship. There is also a suggestion that Wordsworth is using the poem as a kind of coded message to his friend Coleridge, to tell him about the relationship. It was impossible for Wordsworth to talk publicly about his secret love, and their child, because they had never married, and Wordsworth had subsequently married Mary Hutchinson.

BOOK X: RESIDENCE IN FRANCE AND FRENCH REVOLUTION

This continues Wordsworth's reflections on France, and recounts his disillusion with the revolution. He decides to return to England, and then describes his horror and confused emotions as England goes to war with France. He describes his confusion as, whilst staying in the Isle of Wight, he watches the English fleet ready to set sail.

The tone changes dramatically throughout this section.

He is still full of optimism for the revolution and for the freshness of its ideas, which he shares. Gradually, his feelings change, as the situation in France becomes more oppressive. He sees that the revolution is no longer about liberty and freedom, but just about

political power. He becomes even more disillusioned as
similar repressions start to occur in Britain. He becomes
very gloomy and depressed, and is only consoled by the
presence of Dorothy, and, later, by meeting Coleridge.
He begins to feel the healing power of Nature again.
The final part of the poem is written directly to
Coleridge, then in Sicily for his health, although it also
refers to the development of Wordsworth's poetic
mind.

THE FRENCH REVOLUTION (LINES 689–727)

This short section still shows evidence of the optimism
for the revolution, as Wordsworth glories in his own
youth and energy. He feels the world is full of a sense
of hope and promise, and commits himself to seeking
out meaning and pleasure in the world, not in some
imaginary Utopia.

BOOK XI: IMAGINATION, HOW IMPAIRED AND RESTORED

Wordsworth continues his account of his mind, saying
how the disappointment and distress of the reaction to
the revolution has affected him. He wishes for Nature
to restore him, and does feel some consoling power in
the patterns of Nature. At first, he can feel only sensory
pleasure in his surroundings – a little like the feeling he
had in Tintern Abbey, when he was running away from
what he feared- but gradually he starts to feel restored.
He pays tribute to Mary Hutchinson, who has a pure
relationship with Nature, as he had before he left the
Lake District. She is helpful in restoring his faith in
Nature.

Wordsworth
highlights the
key importance
of childhood in
line 276.

An interesting passage starts at line 258, where
Wordsworth discusses 'spots of time'. This is what
he calls key moments in memory, where the mind is
suddenly given an unusually vivid picture of a
particular incident or place. He writes about two of

these 'spots of time'. The first is when, as a very young child (of five years old), he is out riding, and becomes separated from his companion. He sees a gibbet, where a murderer had been hung in years gone by. His name is carved into the grass. Nearby is a pool, where a woman is collecting water. He calls the scene one of 'visionary dreariness', and has clearly never lost the memory of it. The second scene is of three Wordsworth brothers on the lookout for the horses which were to take them home. The wild and stormy weather makes the scene more vivid, but it is the subsequent death of their father which gives the scene real poignancy. Wordsworth closes the book by reflecting on how the mind can return to these special scenes and become restored.

BOOK XII: IMAGINATION, HOW IMPAIRED AND RESTORED (CONTINUED)

The early part of this Book shows Wordsworth coming to terms with the turmoil of emotions he has been through, and once again his faith in human nature is restored.

Nature has taught him once again to respect and care for others. Much of the poem focuses on the delights of the simple life, and rejects the distractions of the overintellectual (just as he had in 'The Tables Turned').

He has become, if anything, convinced of the increased power of Nature to consecrate and transform even the humblest creature. He links the power of Nature and the power of poetry.

Walking around Salisbury plain, he sees Stonehenge and other sights, and these fill him with a sense of history and continuity, as he envisages the past all around him. This section ends with a vision of a 'new

world', which combines the human and the natural in
an equal relationship.

BOOK XIII: CONCLUSION

The final section looks back over what has gone before,
and also looks ahead to the future.

First, he recollects another of the 'spots of time' which
he finds so significant. This takes place on a night
climb of Snowdon, when Wordsworth and his friend
Robert Jones were climbing the mountain accompanied

Intense visual
description is used
to create the
atmosphere here.

by a local shepherd. The journey is without incident,
until suddenly the moon breaks through and illuminates
a great sea of mist around the climbers' feet, while their
heads are in clear, moonlit air. The sight seems magical,
and Wordsworth is able to interpret it as a kind of
image of the flowing and creative power of the
imagination.

Later in this section he pays tribute to Dorothy, for her
faith in him, to his friend Calvert, who left him enough
money to survive on and settle in Dove Cottage, and to
Coleridge, pledging their joint futures to poetry.

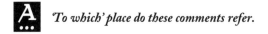

A *'To which' place do these comments refer.*

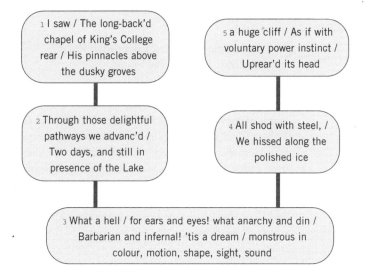

1 I saw / The long-back'd chapel of King's College rear / His pinnacles above the dusky groves

5 a huge cliff / As if with voluntary power instinct / Uprear'd its head

2 Through those delightful pathways we advanc'd / Two days, and still in presence of the Lake

4 All shod with steel, / We hissed along the polished ice

3 What a hell / for ears and eyes! what anarchy and din / Barbarian and infernal! 'tis a dream / monstrous in colour, motion, shape, sight, sound

Check your answers on page 79.

B *Consider these issues.*

a Choose one section of one part of the poem and make detailed notes on it. Try to show what its characteristic features are, and how it relates to other Wordsworth poems. You might like to try this with the 'London Images' section.

a What we learn about Wordsworth's childhood in the first two books which might help us understand his views on poetry.

a Look at some earlier poetry, for example by Pope, and try and imagine how it would have felt to read this for the first time in 1805.

a Look at what *The Prelude* tells us about Wordsworth's relationship with:
i) Dorothy
ii) Coleridge.

a Look closely at one or two sections of *The Prelude*, and consider the way that place is used here compared with earlier poems.

PART THREE

COMMENTARY

THEMES

Wordsworth is a **Romantic** (see Literary Terms) poet, and many of the themes which are typical of Romantic verse in general are important in Wordsworth. Nature is the most obvious of these themes, but the ideas about people are important, too, with Wordsworth having an interest in the individual and the value of individual experience, but also in broader ideas about society. Another theme which is typical of a Romantic poet is the imagination and poetic inspiration. Wordsworth himself was also interested in childhood as an idea. It is also true that there are strong interconnections between themes in Wordsworth, as you will have noticed, so many of the themes overlap somewhat.

NATURE

Changing views of Nature

Nature was, in the late eighteenth and early nineteenth century, seen as something inspiring and beautiful, especially in its wild, untamed state. A common word applied to Nature and natural objects was '**sublime**' (see Literary Terms). This implied a sense of awe and wonder, and was closely connected with the idea of the imagination of the individual poet. This sense contrasted with the earlier eighteenth century, when Nature was seen as something very much to be brought under human control.

Wordsworth and Nature

For Wordsworth, Nature was a starting point in his own life and in his poetry. Many characters (Lucy, the Old Cumberland Beggar, the man in 'Animal Tranquillity and Decay', the child in 'We are Seven') are seen as being at one with Nature, and for Wordsworth the poet this is a very pure state. It is also, to an extent, an unattainable state, which for him existed only in childhood. In 'Nutting', and in the early books of *The Prelude*, and in his memory of his first visit to Tintern Abbey, we see descriptions of the youthful Wordsworth's response to Nature – he really feels passionate and intense. As he gets older he is aware that the way he feels changes to the more measured, calm response which he describes later in 'Tintern Abbey', and in 'Expostulation and Reply' / 'Tables Turned'. Now Nature works through memory to calm and soothe. He feels devastated by the loss of this intensity, but tries to come to terms with it.

Nature as a teacher

We see vividly in Book I of *The Prelude*, how Nature (Wordsworth said he was 'led by her') teaches the over-confident young William a lesson in her power, and strikes fear into his heart when he steals the boat. Nature also adopts and teaches the pure character of Lucy, which both emphasises Lucy's purity and goodness, but also signals her death, as the ultimate way of getting close to Nature. Although many people might now describe Wordsworth as a 'nature poet', in fact he does not really concentrate much on close-up details of natural description. Instead, he is more concerned with the interaction between people and Nature, and particularly between himself and Nature. These thoughts are most obvious in 'Tintern Abbey' and *The Prelude*.

Nature and humans

Poems such as 'Expostulation and Reply' illustrate something very specific in Wordsworth's views about the close connection between humans and Nature, almost an **animistic** (see Literary Terms) sense of something we both share, but which humans need to try to achieve (it comes naturally to wild objects). Wordsworth often writes as if wild objects (e.g. leaves) can feel things which we would normally think of as human emotions. Here he is not simply **personifying** (see Literary Terms) objects. Instead he is trying to suggest some very deep connection between the human and the natural.

PEOPLE

People on the edge of society

We think of our era as a time of change – technology moving rapidly, new media developing, and the Romantic (see Literary Terms) period was just as exciting. Many of the changes of the Agricultural and early pre-Industrial revolution were reflected in Wordsworth's poems.

Later poets (notably Shelley) mocked Wordsworth for his increasing conservatism as he got older, but many of his poems are used to show the poor state, but essential humanity, of many country people and also to show how others could learn from the kind of marginal existence of these people. To use a modern phrase in a literal sense, these people are on the edge. The fragile but plucky Simon Lee is a good example. Poor Susan, separated from the things and places she loves is another. In 'Michael', the family are shown as being isolated from the rest of the community, and this contributes to the poignancy of their final tragedy. You will notice that the earlier poems tend to be most concerned with these issues.

Poverty and isolated individuals

Many of the poems describe poverty-stricken individuals and Wordsworth has a rather ambiguous attitude to them. He sees them as close to Nature, at one with Nature. At the same time, this same closeness is impossible for him, so, although his poetry allows him to come close to their experience, it also makes him see the gap between himself and them.

People and landscape

Closely connected with the above idea is the notion of the relationship between people and their environment. For Wordsworth it is vitally important that people feel they can connect with the place they live, and fit in to their landscape. The kind of **dissonance** (see Literary Terms) and pain felt by Poor Susan is a good example of what happens when people are separated from the places they belong to. It is interesting to see, too, how often Wordsworth locates characters in a specific place, often within a very local environment. It is also interesting to note that although, in 'I Travelled Among Unknown Men' and in parts of *The Prelude*, he himself bemoans the fact that he has been away and wishes to return to his beloved Lakes, the times that he was away, particularly in Goslar, Germany, were some of his most creative. Perhaps this shows that some people need to go away from their environment in order to truly feel its power. Other characters, though, (think of Michael, Lucy) are so strongly associated with their personal landscape that it would be impossible to imagine them anywhere else.

Look back at Resolution and Independence *for another good example.*

Individual experience

The Romantic period marked the start of one aspect of what we might see as our modern consciousness – the valuing of individual experience. This is expressed most powerfully, of course, in *The Prelude* (remember its subtitle: 'The Growth of a Poet's Mind'). Many other Wordsworth poems also show a prioritising of the experience of the individual, sometimes as a way of commenting on society, but most often it is simply to make us focus on the special insights that one individual can give us. This is most obviously the case with characters who are suffering mental disturbance, such as in 'The Idiot Boy', or 'The Thorn'. It is also true of many other characters.

INSPIRATION

The idea that poetry came through inspiration, rather than simple technical skill, was a crucial theme in **Romantic** (see Literary Terms) thought. The whole of

The Prelude is, in some ways, an analysis of how inspiration comes about.

The
imagination

This is one of the key concepts in Romantic thought. Wordsworth observed how the imagination could develop from the exciting, fresh, but possibly destructive force of 'Nutting' and the first visit to Tintern Abbey, to the more controlled force of the later 'Tintern Abbey' and The Prelude. Nature is the prime force which inspires, through beauty, grandeur or a

This idea could be
summed up in 'A
Slumber did my
Spirit Seal' (Lucy
Poems).

sense of the **sublime** (see Literary Terms). Intensity of human experience can also inspire, such as in the poems of poverty-stricken individuals. Interestingly, Wordsworth himself, in his poetry, tended to shy away from writing about intense experience in his own private life, though he is happy to write of strong reactions to Nature, friendships and more abstract concepts. The Vaudracour and Julia story in Book IX of The Prelude is the closest he comes to writing of his own love for Annette Vallon, and though Mary Hutchinson, who became his wife, is often mentioned, it is with less intensity than more abstract ideas.

CHILDHOOD

Childhood innocence plays an important role in many of Wordsworth's poems, and it is often contrasted with adult cynicism. The best example of this is in 'We are Seven', when Wordsworth shows us the arrogance of the narrator, thinking he knows better than the little girl.

'The child is
father of the
man'

The other important idea about childhood in Wordsworth is the way in which your childhood experiences prepare you for adult life. This is in many ways a modern view, similar to what psychoanalysts believe in the twentieth century. The key poem here, is of course The Prelude, where Wordsworth looks back on

his life to see how he became a poet. 'Nutting' is also
interesting in this way. 'The Idiot Boy' takes childhood
innocence a stage further, emphasising the intensity of
experience which an innocent can achieve.

FORM

It is obvious from the use of the title *Lyrical Ballads*
that Wordsworth was very interested in the form (see
Literary Terms) of poems, and often experimented. At
the time of *Lyrical Ballads*, for instance, he was trying
to change the way poetry was perceived. He wanted to
make poetry accessible to people who had not before
been the assumed audience. This was why he chose to
use forms which were like the songs and rhymes which
ordinary country people would know.

*Lyrical
Ballads*

The simple lyrical form of poems like the 'Lucy Poems',
or 'Lucy Gray', show how very simple forms and
language can be used to express strong and often
abstract emotions. Wordsworth was often criticised for
poems like 'Goody Blake and Harry Gill', and, of
course, 'The Thorn', but it is in these poems that his
experiments are most evident to us now. The strong
rhymes, especially that famous rhyming couplet at the
end of stanza III (see Literary Terms) in 'The Thorn',

*Notice how the
voice of the
narrator is always
reflected in their
style of speech.*

are techniques which have always been used in popular
narrative verse. Wordsworth, in many of these poems,
is trying to recreate the voices of people who have not
appeared in poetry as voices or as real characters before,
so the form he chooses is especially important.

Abstract ideas

More complex poems, which try to address complex
thought as well as emotion, notably 'Tintern Abbey'
and *The Prelude* are written in blank verse (see Literary
Terms), which has traditionally been used for this sort
of theme. Wordsworth was a great admirer of the poets

Shakespeare and Milton, who were both great users of this and the following form.

Sonnets The sonnet (see Literary Terms) is a highly structured form, with strict rules. Instead of restricting the poet, these rules can provide a discipline for the great poet, who can make use of the form to its best effect.

Many sonnets consist of an octet (eight lines) followed by a sestet (six lines) (see Literary Terms). You can see the use of the form very clearly in 'Composed Upon Westminster Bridge', where the first eight lines paint a broad picture of the whole scene. Then, in the final sestet, the focus changes to the poet's reaction, and this is how the poem concludes.

Wordsworth wrote many sonnets later in his career.

Other forms In the 'Intimations' Ode, Wordsworth deliberately chooses a form which goes right back to Classical times. The Ode form allows him to be flexible about the arrangement of individual stanzas, but to still keep a sense of unity in the poem as a whole.

LANGUAGE & STYLE

Like every poet, Wordsworth was acutely concerned to use appropriate diction (see Literary Terms) for the purpose and subject of each poem.

Often, for Wordsworth, the appropriate language was connected with the characters of the poem. A good example is the innocent way the child speaks in 'We Are Seven', or the rather wordy style of the narrator in 'The Thorn'.

Everyday speech In the Preface to the *Lyrical Ballads*, Wordsworth wrote of the need to write in the language of 'everyday speech'. That is to say, he and Coleridge were making

an effort to turn away from traditional poetic language.
So, in poems like 'Goody Blake and Harry Gill' and
'The Idiot Boy', Wordsworth deliberately uses local
colloquialisms (see Literary Terms) to give the poem a
more vivid and realistic feeling. The form of the poems
has a similar effect (see Form and Literary Terms).

Imagery

Because of Wordsworth's interest in making poetry
accessible, imagery (see Literary Terms) is often not an
important part of his writing. If you look, for example,
at the 'Lucy Poem' – 'She Dwelt Among the
Untrodden Ways' – much of the expression is
straightforward or even prosaic, for example:

> A Maid whom there were none to praise
> And very few to love:

Sometimes
imagery can
suggest several
interpretations,
e.g. 'The Thorn'.

As you might expect, much of the imagery in
Wordsworth's poetry is drawn from Nature, and you
can see this in the same poem. When Lucy is described,
she is compared to objects within the natural world, for
example, she is 'A violet by a mossy stone', or 'Fair as a
star'.

This very spare and deliberately limited use of language
in the shorter poems makes it all the more striking
when he does diverge from this simple vocabulary. In
'A Slumber did my Spirit Seal', the use of 'diurnal'
which is a rather complex and scientific word is
certainly surprising and almost shocking.

Longer poems, such as *The Prelude* tend to be richer in
imagery, though its source is still the natural world:

> I wheeled about,
> Proud and exulting, like an untired horse,
> That cares not for its home. (Book I, lines 458–60)

In the longer poems, and 'Tintern Abbey' is a good
example of this, diction may also be deliberately more
complex and demanding and perhaps more consciously
poetic.

PART FOUR

STUDY SKILLS

HOW TO USE QUOTATIONS

One of the secrets of success in writing essays is the way you use quotations. There are five basic principles:

- Put inverted commas at the beginning and end of the quotation
- Write the quotation exactly as it appears in the original
- Do not use a quotation that repeats what you have just written
- Use the quotation so that it fits into your sentence
- Keep the quotation as short as possible

Quotations should be used to develop the line of thought in your essays.

Your comment should not duplicate what is in your quotation. For example:

In 'The Tables Turned', Wordsworth describes how our human minds can distort the beauty of Nature. He says, 'Our meddling intellect / Mis-shapes the beauteous forms of things'.

Far more effective is to write:

In 'The Tables Turned' Wordsworth demonstrates the destructive effects of the human mind: 'Our meddling intellect', which 'Mis-shapes the beauteous forms of things'.

Always lay out the lines as they appear in the text. For example:

The narrator uses natural images to describe Lucy. She is 'A violet by a mossy stone / Half hidden from the eye!'

However, the most sophisticated way of using the writer's words is to embed them into your sentence:

The natural images of the 'violet' next to the 'mossy stone' and the 'star' all remind us of Lucy's close connection with Nature.

When you use quotations in this way, you are demonstrating the ability to use text as evidence to support your ideas - not simply including words from the original to prove you have read it.

Everyone writes differently. Work through the suggestions given here and adapt the advice to suit your own style and interests. This will improve your essay-writing skills and allow your personal voice to emerge.

The following points indicate in ascending order the skills of essay writing:
- Picking out one or two facts about the story and adding the odd detail
- Writing about the text by retelling the story
- Retelling the story and adding a quotation here and there
- Organising an answer which explains what is happening in the text and giving quotations to support what you write

....

- Writing in such a way as to show that you have thought about the intentions of the writer of the text and that you understand the techniques used
- Writing at some length, giving your viewpoint on the text and commenting by picking out details to support your views
- Looking at the text as a work of art, demonstrating clear critical judgement and explaining to the reader of your essay how the enjoyment of the text is assisted by literary devices, linguistic effects and psychological insights; showing how the text relates to the time when it was written

The dotted line above represents the division between lower and higher level grades. Higher-level performance begins when you start to consider your response as a reader of the text. The highest level is reached when you offer an enthusiastic personal response and show how this piece of literature is a product of its time.

Coursework
essay

Set aside an hour or so at the start of your work to plan what you have to do.

- List all the points you feel are needed to cover the task. Collect page references of information and quotations that will support what you have to say. A helpful tool is the highlighter pen: this saves painstaking copying and enables you to target precisely what you want to use.
- Focus on what you consider to be the main points of the essay. Try to sum up your argument in a single sentence, which could be the closing sentence of your essay. Depending on the essay title, it could be a subject of the poem: In 'Tintern Abbey' Wordsworth shows us how the mind's reactions to nature develop over time; an opinion about setting: The thorn bush, the pond and the heap of moss combine to create a symbolic background to Martha Ray's tragedy in 'The Thorn'; or a judgement on a theme: In 'Nutting', the complex relationship between people and Nature emerges as the main theme'.
- Make a short essay plan. Use the first paragraph to introduce the argument you wish to make. In the following paragraphs develop this argument with details, examples and other possible points of view. Sum up your argument in the last paragraph. Check you have answered the question.
- Write the essay, remembering all the time the central point you are making.
- On completion, go back over what you have written to eliminate careless errors and improve expression. Read it aloud to yourself, or, if you are feeling more confident, to a relative or friend.

If you can, try to type your essay, using a word processor. This will allow you to correct and improve your writing without spoiling its appearance.

Examination
essay

The essay written in an examination often carries more marks than the coursework essay even though it is written under considerable time pressure.

In the revision period build up notes on various aspects of the text you are using. Fortunately, in acquiring this set of York Notes on *William Wordsworth Selected Poems*, you have made a prudent beginning! York Notes are set out to give you vital information and help you to construct your personal overview of the text.

Make notes with appropriate quotations about the key issues of the set text. Go into the examination knowing your text and having a clear set of opinions about it.

In most English Literature examinations you can take in copies of your set books. This in an enormous advantage although it may lull you into a false sense of security. Beware! There is simply not enough time in an examination to read the book from scratch.

In the
examination

- Read the question paper carefully and remind yourself what you have to do.
- Look at the questions on your set texts to select the one that most interests you and mentally work out the points you wish to stress.
- Remind yourself of the time available and how you are going to use it.
- Briefly map out a short plan in note form that will keep your writing on track and illustrate the key argument you want to make.
- Then set about writing it.
- When you have finished, check through to eliminate errors.

To summarise,
these are the
keys to success:

- **Know the text**
- **Have a clear understanding of and opinions on the storyline, characters, setting, themes and writer's concerns**
- **Select the right material**
- **Plan and write a clear response, continually bearing the question in mind**

SAMPLE ESSAY PLAN

A typical essay question on *William Wordsworth Selected Poems* is followed by a sample essay plan in note form. This does not present the only answer to the question, merely one. Always try to use your own ideas.

Discuss Wordsworth's different attitudes to Nature in a selection of his poems.

Part 1
Introduction
- Context of Romantic attitudes to Nature
- Contrast with earlier eighteenth century
- Variety within Wordsworth (e.g. from 'Lines Written in Early Spring' to 'Intimations' Ode)

Part 2
- Sublime/inspirational in Nature ('Tintern Abbey', 'Lines Written in Early Spring')
- Earlier poems tend to concentrate on beauty and sublimity, but also
- Nature as teacher ('Lucy Poems', *The Prelude* Book I)
- Nature linked to specific personalities – as background (e.g. 'The Thorn', 'Michael')
- Nature has special link to poor ('Animal Tranquillity and Decay')
- Nature can be inspiring and consoling even when we are far away ('Poor Susan', 'Tintern Abbey')
- Nature can even exist as an inspiration in the city ('Composed upon Westminster Bridge')

Part 3
But
- Wordsworth can sometimes feel excluded from the sense of harmony in Nature ('Intimations' Ode)

And
- Human love is also important (*The Prelude*, 'Tintern Abbey' 'She was a Phantom of Delight')

Conclusion
- Wordsworth brought Nature into poetry in a new and fresh way. This is shown by the many parts Nature plays in his poems. At the same time, we should remember that what was important was not just Nature, but our human relationships within it.

Make a plan as shown above and attempt these questions:

1 Discuss the role of women in Wordsworth's poetry.
2 What development over time can you observe in Wordsworth's poetry?
3 Choose one poem from the collection that you have enjoyed, and say how it is typical (or not!) of the rest of his poetry.
4 Using three or more poems, discuss what you think Wordsworth had to say about childhood.
5 Wordsworth's poems contain many memorable characters. Choose one of these, and write a short monologue (or journal) in their voice. For example, you might choose Martha Ray ('The Thorn'), Luke (the son in 'Michael'), Goody Blake or Harry Gill (or both!).
6 Imagine what the story behind 'The Thorn' might be. What really happened? Tell the story from Martha's point of view.
7 Write about the character of Lucy. Discuss how she is presented in different poems.
8 Lucy Poems IV and V are written in a very simple verse form. Invent a contemporary character and write a series of short poems about them, showing them in different ways each time. Experiment with using a narrator, too.
9 Look at 'The Idiot Boy'. Discuss the mother/son relationship in this poem.

PART FIVE

CULTURAL CONNECTIONS

BROADER PERSPECTIVES

By now you will have some idea of what the Romantic (see Literary Terms) movement was all about, and what role Wordsworth played in the early days.

Before Lyr· ·l Ballads   Two important poets who had an influence on Romantic poetry were writing just before *Lyrical Ballads*, and are both seen as being on the fringes of the Romantic movement, Robert Burns, the Scottish poet, and William Blake, whose *Songs of Innocence and Experience* (1794) bears many similarities to *Lyrical Ballads*, in the way he uses simple, accessible forms (see Literary Terms).

Contemporaries   Coleridge, as has been mentioned throughout these Notes, was writing at the same time as Wordsworth. The two poets worked together on *Lyrical Ballads*, and Coleridge's major contribution, *The Rime of the Ancient Mariner* (1798), makes an interesting parallel read. Coleridge is more interested in the spiritual and supernatural than Wordsworth, and this is evident in this poem.

Later Romantics   You might want to follow up Wordsworth's interest in political ideas by reading Shelley's poems, such as the sonnet *Ozymandias* (1818), or the much longer *Mask of Anarchy* (1819). Shelley also wrote a humorous poem making fun of Wordsworth, in *Peter Bell the third* (1819). Poems by Keats and Byron give a good sense of how ideas about Romantic writing and the Romantic imagination developed.

Novels   Some of the key Romantic ideas of passion, terror and the sublime (see Literary Terms) are to be found in novels of the same period, such as the Gothic Horror of

Matthew Lewis's *The Monk* (1796) or Horace Walpole's *The Castle of Otranto* (1764). Probably the most famous novel of the Romantic period is Mary Shelley's *Frankenstein* (1818) which again contains ideas of terror, but also includes thoughts on the power of imagination and creativity. Kenneth Branagh's film, *Mary Shelley's Frankenstein* (1994) gives a flavour of some of the ideas.

Other prose   One of the best writers to read in conjunction with William Wordsworth is his sister, Dorothy. Her journals (begun in 1798) give a good insight into the creative and the domestic life at this time. The edition *Home at Grasmere* combines her writing with some of William's poetry.

alliteration repetition of consonants at the beginning of a sequence of words such as 'broken bough' in 'Nutting'

animism giving the idea of a living soul to plants, etc

assonance rhyming of vowels only ('feel' and 'need')

autobiography a book telling the story of the life of its subject, written by its subject. Wordsworth's *The Prelude* is the most important example of a poetic autobiography

ballad/lyrical ballad a ballad is a simple poem, familiar or accessible to ordinary people, and often set to music. It usually has a very simple form, often in 4-line stanzas, containing alternate rhymes. A lyric was originally a song, or a song-like poem, but came to mean poems that were expressive of the poet's emotions

blank verse the form Wordsworth used for *The Prelude*. Lines normally consist of 10 syllables, with an iambic rhythm (one lightly stressed syllable, one strongly stressed). It was the rhythm popular in Shakespeare

colloquial use of language which is informal or casual, e.g. the use of dialect words in 'The Idiot Boy'

couplet a pair of lines, usually rhymed, e.g.

At the corner of Wood street, when daylight appears,

Hangs a Thrush that sings loud, it has sung for three years:

'The Reverie of Poor Susan'

diction refers to the choice of words the poet uses. Diction may be prosaic (the language of prose, or everyday language), or poetic (when we think of poetry, we often expect poets to use extravagant or old-fashioned language)

dissonance disagreement or lack of harmony

form refers to the arrangement and structure of poems, for example, the length of lines and the way the poem is divided up into stanzas

imagery language in which similes and metaphors are used. More generally, the word is used to cover all words appealing to the senses or feelings

metaphor figure of speech in which something is spoken of as being what it resembles, e.g. the stones in 'Nutting' are 'fleeced with moss'

metre regulated succession of groups of syllables creating a pattern. It is based on the use of long and short or stressed and unstressed syllables

monosyllable a word of one syllable (e.g. 'yes' or 'no')

octet the first group of eight lines, linked by rhyme in a sonnet. Followed by a sestet

onomatopoeia use of words whose sound helps to suggest the meaning, such as 'rushed' and 'pattered' in 'A Whirl-Blast from behind the hill'

pastoral originally pastoral poetry described an ideal version of the countryside as a sort of escapism. Later pastorals became a little more realistic

personify to give inanimate objects the qualities of humans

quatrain a group or stanza of four lines, usually linked by rhyme. Frequently used in ballads

rhythm variation in the level of stress placed on syllables in a poem

romantic refers to a particular period and style of literature, typified by an interest in dramatic natural scenes and equally dramatic and extreme emotions

sestet the group of six lines which conclude a sonnet

simile an image using a direct comparison, for instance 'holy time is quiet as a Nun' in 'It is a Beauteous Evening'

stanza an individual section of the poem, which the poet has chosen to separate from others. Sometimes referred to as verses, especially in simpler poems

sublime a word used specifically in relation to Romantic poetry, meaning an adjective which describes the stunning and spectacular vision of Nature

versification the way a poet manipulates verse form or length for different effects

TEST ANSWERS

TEST YOURSELF (Section I)

A 1 The thorn bush *('The Thorn')*
2 William *('Expostulation and Reply')*
3 Simon Lee *('Simon Lee')*
4 The little girl *('We are Seven')*
5 Goody Blake *('Goody Blake and Harry Gill')*
6 The narrator *('Lines Written in Early Spring')*

TEST YOURSELF (Section II)

A 1 Lucy *('I Travelled Among Unknown Men'* in the *'Lucy Poems')*
2 Lucy Gray *('Lucy Gray')*
3 The boy *('Nutting')*
4 Michael *('Michael')*
5 The Leech Gatherer *('Resolution and Independence')*
6 Luke, the son *('Michael')*

TEST YOURSELF (Section III)

A 1 Mary Hutchinson, Wordsworth's wife *('She was a Phantom of Delight')*
2 The Solitary Reaper *('The Solitary Reaper')*
3 Caroline Vallon, Wordsworth's daughter *('It is a Beauteous Evening')*
4 The child *('Intimations' Ode – Stanza VII)*

TEST YOURSELF (Section IV: The Prelude)

A 1 Cambridge *(Book III,* lines 4–5)
2 In Italy, walking in the Alps *(Book VI,* lines 617–8)
3 St Bartholomew's Fair, London, *(Book VII,* lines 658–70)
4 Skating, in the Lake District *(Book I,* lines 460–1)
5 The famous boating incident, in the Lake District. Wordsworth suggests it is at Patterdale, so the lake is probably Ullswater.

GCSE and equivalent levels (£3.50 each)

Maya Angelou
I Know Why the Caged Bird Sings

Jane Austen
Pride and Prejudice

Alan Ayckbourn
Absent Friends

Elizabeth Barrett Browning
Selected Poems

Robert Bolt
A Man for All Seasons

Harold Brighouse
Hobson's Choice

Charlotte Brontë
Jane Eyre

Emily Brontë
Wuthering Heights

Shelagh Delaney
A Taste of Honey

Charles Dickens
David Copperfield

Charles Dickens
Great Expectations

Charles Dickens
Hard Times

Charles Dickens
Oliver Twist

Roddy Doyle
Paddy Clarke Ha Ha Ha

George Eliot
Silas Marner

George Eliot
The Mill on the Floss

William Golding
Lord of the Flies

Oliver Goldsmith
She Stoops To Conquer

Willis Hall
The Long and the Short and the Tall

Thomas Hardy
Far from the Madding Crowd

Thomas Hardy
The Mayor of Casterbridge

Thomas Hardy
Tess of the d'Urbervilles

Thomas Hardy
The Withered Arm and other Wessex Tales

L.P. Hartley
The Go-Between

Seamus Heaney
Selected Poems

Susan Hill
I'm the King of the Castle

Barry Hines
A Kestrel for a Knave

Louise Lawrence
Children of the Dust

Harper Lee
To Kill a Mockingbird

Laurie Lee
Cider with Rosie

Arthur Miller
The Crucible

Arthur Miller
A View from the Bridge

Robert O'Brien
Z for Zachariah

Frank O'Connor
My Oedipus Complex and other stories

George Orwell
Animal Farm

J.B. Priestley
An Inspector Calls

Willy Russell
Educating Rita

Willy Russell
Our Day Out

J.D. Salinger
The Catcher in the Rye

William Shakespeare
Henry IV Part 1

William Shakespeare
Henry V

William Shakespeare
Julius Caesar

William Shakespeare
Macbeth

William Shakespeare
The Merchant of Venice

William Shakespeare
A Midsummer Night's Dream

William Shakespeare
Much Ado About Nothing

William Shakespeare
Romeo and Juliet

William Shakespeare
The Tempest

William Shakespeare
Twelfth Night

George Bernard Shaw
Pygmalion

Mary Shelley
Frankenstein

R.C. Sherriff
Journey's End

Rukshana Smith
Salt on the snow

John Steinbeck
Of Mice and Men

Robert Louis Stevenson
Dr Jekyll and Mr Hyde

Jonathan Swift
Gulliver's Travels

Robert Swindells
Daz 4 Zoe

Mildred D. Taylor
Roll of Thunder, Hear My Cry

Mark Twain
Huckleberry Finn

James Watson
Talking in Whispers

William Wordsworth
Selected Poems

A Choice of Poets

Mystery Stories of the Nineteenth Century including The Signalman

Nineteenth Century Short Stories

Poetry of the First World War

Six Women Poets